HOW TO ACE YOUR (UNDERGRAD) ECONOMICS DISSERTATION

A SHORT AND COMPREHENSIVE SURVIVAL GUIDE

EDWARD WELLINGTON

PREFACE: WORK HARD (AND SMART)

This is a quick and comprehensive guidebook on how to write an undergraduate economics dissertation successfully. It is purposely written shortly and succinctly - yes, I was once a student too and I know that no one has the time to read through lengthy texts! Well, good news because this guidebook will get straight to the point.

So, you may be reading this guidebook right now because you have an upcoming economics thesis in the next semester(s), or you may have even started writing it. In this book, I will provide you with a step-by-step guide on how to ACE your economics dissertation without putting in excessive amounts of effort. Is this too good to be true? An 'A' without much effort? Well, no of course you have to put in SOME effort, but you need not slave your life away for a good grade on your economics dissertation. *The secret to doing well is working smart, and that's equally as important as working hard.* I realize, however, that many students often neglect the former! This is why this guidebook is written - to (hopefully) motivate YOU to work SMART and excel in your economics dissertation.

Throughout the years as an economics teaching assistant and professor, I've come to realize that many students also undervalue the importance of their final year thesis projects and are eager to get it 'over and done with'. Do not adopt the same mindset! *Final year dissertations are called capstone projects for a reason. They, directly and indirectly, prepare you for landing your first serious job out of university.* In my years of experience in the job market (both in the private and public sectors), interviewers have asked about my undergraduate economics dissertation about 50% of the time. Times have changed. We do not live in our parents' era when dissertations were not always required for a degree. It is also likely that your interviewer had to write a dissertation, and is interested in what you did for yours. Even if you do not get asked about your thesis topic, it is useful to draw from what you had done in your dissertation to answer some of the interview questions. Not only could this help to improve the quality and depth of the interview, but it would also show that you are capable of conducting research independently. And that, my friend, is a very valuable asset.

In the world of academia, the quality of an economics research paper is mainly determined by three factors: 1). Originality and Contribution, 2). Data and 3). Empirical Method (for quantitative papers) or Conceptual Framework (for theoretical papers). So yes, in essence, your economics dissertation grade will mostly depend on these three main indicators. This book, therefore, goes into these topics in greater detail to help you 'optimize' your economics dissertation grade. Do not skip these sections, or you will regret it!

Just one more note before we get started with the guidebook. *Another common misconception among students is that statistically significant results are the most important.* But, depending on the nature and topic of your study, this may not necessarily be the case. Say, for instance, your study finds that giving poorer households cash transfers had a statistically *insignificant* effect on their children's nutrition. What does this tell you? Does it mean your results are 'bad'? In this example, the answer is no. In fact, these results are interesting for your examiner because this indicates that cash transfers are not a useful method for improving poor children's health and nutrition. From a policy perspective, this means that cash transfer programs should either be accompanied by other interventions to improve poor children's health or that other interventions that target children's health outcomes should be considered instead. So, do not discard statistically insignificant results immediately! Stop and think carefully about why your results are insignificant and how these findings could be interesting for your paper.

To make the most use of this quick guidebook, go through each section *consecutively*. By this, I mean do not skip through sections and follow the flow of the book. It is written and structured in a way that will help you to write a successful economics dissertation. *Let me also emphasize the importance of planning your dissertation before starting it!* Many students underestimate the power of planning, organizing, and structuring their dissertations before beginning. Planning your economics dissertation before starting is among one of the biggest determinants of your final grade. So, be sure to carefully follow the steps in this guidebook to help you plan out your dissertation!

DEDICATION

For all of my Economics undergraduate students undertaking their final capstone projects, and to my 22-year old former self, where I was once an undergraduate Honors Economics student at the University of Western Ontario (UWO). I also dedicate this book to UWO's Economics class of 2015 - I dare say we are the best (and most successful) cohort our professors had.

DISCLAIMER

This guidebook does not guarantee any specific grade on students' economics dissertations. It should be treated as a reference book to complement students' economics lectures and assignment notes. It is important to know that dissertation grades depend on many factors such as the nature of the study, students' dedication and capabilities, examiner's perspective, among others.

TABLE OF CONTENTS

CHAPTER 1

EMPIRICAL VS. THEORETICAL DISSERTATIONS: WHICH TO PICK?

A). Calculus vs. Statistics. Which are you better at or are interested in? If your answer is calculus, you could consider a theoretical paper. If it is statistics, go for an empirical study. If it is neither, go for an empirical study. Yes, I generally recommend that students do an empirical paper. Why is this so? First, the number of theoretical papers in economics has dwindled over the years, not because it is less important, but because data has become more widely available these days to conduct meaningful empirical studies. After all, what's the point of economic theory if you do not use real-life data to prove it? Second, theoretical papers can become tedious, especially when it comes to mathematical proofs, so unless you are into these sorts of topics, think twice before going for a theoretical dissertation, or else you may end up spending longer than you wish on your thesis. Third, empirical studies allow you to apply your econometrics and statistical knowledge to real-world situations. This means that if you intend to go for a job with a more quantitative role for example, your empirical paper will be very beneficial as it allows you to apply your statistics and econometrics knowledge to real-world data.

However, note that while empirical studies have grown in popularity, this does not mean that they do not draw from economic models and theories. *It is extremely important to refer to economic*

1

models or theories to explain your empirical findings. So, while you may have written an empirical paper, you should always relate your results to economic theory! Well-written economics papers always use economic theory to back up their quantitative findings. Therefore, if you want an 'A' grade, this is something you must do and should not neglect.

B). What type of skills do you wish to gain? Your economics thesis is supposed to prepare you for your interviews and jobs post-college. *So think carefully about what you would like to gain from this dissertation writing journey*. If you are absolutely in love with economic theory, or are a genius at calculus and would like to build your academic career based on theoretical work, then a theoretical paper is for you. To clarify what I mean by academic career, I mean if you have the aspiration to become a professor. Personally, I did not write a theoretical paper for my undergraduate economics thesis and here I am today.

In essence, what I am saying is that if going into academia is not what you want, an empirical paper would be much more useful for you. This is because the skills you gain from doing an empirical study are much more relevant to the demands of the labor market. Because you will have to learn to use statistical packages like STATA or other equivalent programs like R, SPSS, Python, Gretl, or Eviews, your chances of getting hired in today's highly competitive job market are likely to be higher if you know how to use these programs! And, it's even better if you know how to use these programs to analyze real-world data. An empirical economics dissertation is therefore the best way to perfect your statistical programming skills before starting your job search.

CHAPTER 2

PRACTICALITY VS. PASSION

Students should pick economics dissertation topics they are *passionate* about because passion and interest are significant determinants of success. However, it is also beneficial to be *practical* in your topic choice. It is very important to think about what matters to you more in your economics dissertation writing journey. Is writing about something you are genuinely interested in more important than writing about a topic that is easier to 'sell'? What I mean by this, for example, is that Macroeconomics is much more widely understood in the private sector or labor market, than say Agricultural Economics. So, while you may be slightly more interested in writing an Agricultural Economics study, your future employer at a financial firm, for instance, may be less likely to be able to relate to your thesis.

This may not seem like a big deal if you do not get asked about your economics dissertation at a job interview. But, even so, your thesis topic would come in very handy when writing cover letters or talking about yourself at job interviews. Given that you might not have had much work experience before graduating, drawing from your previous academic experiences such as capstone projects like your economics dissertation is crucial.

At the end of the day, ask yourself what's more important to you. Having a slightly 'easier' time landing a job after college, or doing what you love by writing about a topic you are passionate about? *The best advice is to find a middle ground.* Try to come up with a topic that you are more or less interested in, and one that would be relevant for your future career prospects and aspirations.

CHAPTER 3

ZOOMING IN

Once you have decided on an economics discipline, it is time to zoom into exactly what it is about this field of economics that you want to write about in your dissertation. Now how do you do this?

A). Think about the common issues in your discipline of choice. Say, for example, you choose Development Economics, where poverty, health, education, and gender, are all major topics in development, among others. Or, if you select Labor Economics, gender wage gaps, youth unemployment rates, child labor, are also pressing issues that are worth considering.

B). Is there a question, or are there questions within these issues you have always wanted the answer to? For instance, have you always wondered whether cash transfer programs (i.e. giving an unconditional sum of money to poor individuals or households) are effective in alleviating poverty and improving the nutritional outcomes of children? Or, have you thought about why youth unemployment rates are so high in countries like Tanzania? *Always draw from your own curiosity to build a research question* because this is a huge motivating factor for your dissertation.

C). Which geographic region are you interested in examining, and is your research question relevant to that region? If you want to study a developed country like the U.S. or Canada, are cash transfers applicable in these contexts? Not as much as they are in less-developed regions, where poverty is more rampant. Therefore, you may have to change the region or country you are interested in to answer your research question appropriately. Another example is the topic of mining. For instance, you may want to examine the effect of copper mining on the health outcomes of newborns. However, not all countries or regions are geologically endowed with copper. Your dissertation should thus aim to answer this research question in the context of a copper-rich country or geographic area where this question may be more relevant.

D). How will this topic or discipline in economics help with your future career prospects and aspirations? What do you want to do after your studies? If you wish to become a social scientist, work at a non-governmental organization (NGO) or inter-governmental organization (IGO), *how interesting is your thesis topic for this future employer? Is it relevant to the work that they do?* In summary, it is important to ask these questions to help you narrow your research topic down.

CHAPTER 4

CONTRIBUTION AND ORIGINALITY

Once you've narrowed down on your research question(s), think about the following:

A). Has this research question already been answered in existing studies? If so, how concerned are you with 'sacrificing' some marks due to unoriginality and lack of contribution? This component should account for approximately 10-15% of your dissertation grade, depending on your university. Some universities may put even more emphasis on this component (up to 20%!). Based on your level of concern, you might want to go back and think of a more unique research question that has not been explored in existing economic literature. Otherwise, is there another research question *similar* to your topic of choice but has not been examined yet? Or, is it possible to answer this research question in the context of a *different geographical location*? If so, these are some ways to work around studies that have already been done before, including some suggestions below.

B). In what way does your research paper contribute to existing studies? For example, does your paper use *novel data* that no other studies have used before to answer the research question, or is your study the *first to identify a causal impact* of cash transfers on the health outcomes of poor children in Nigeria, for instance? Do you also adopt a *new empirical method* that has not been used before in other studies? These are more ways a paper can contribute to existing literature,

7

among others, and it is important to emphasize how your dissertation uniquely adds to present studies on the topic.

C). Think about why your study is significant and how it benefits a particular group or society. For instance, say you find that firm performance increases with a female CEO, what does this imply? It indicates that a CEO's gender is an important factor in determining the performance of a firm and that companies should be more supportive of women in top management or C-level functions. Or, what if your results show that cash transfers have a statistically *insignificant* effect on the nutritional status of poor children in Nigeria? Because health and nutrition are highly correlated with educational performance and attendance, which in turn influence future labor market outcomes, this finding implies that cash transfers are a futile intervention for improving the health outcomes of children from poorer households and alleviating long-run poverty. In essence, *think about how the findings from your paper can help improve society or benefit particular socio-demographic groups.*

CHAPTER 5

STRUCTURE AND ORGANIZATION

M any students often neglect the importance of this section. I would argue that *proper structure and organization of your thesis is one of the most crucial determinants of a successful economics dissertation.* Why is this so? A research paper that is badly planned and organized makes it difficult for the examiner to follow the writer's thought process. As a result, the study will be undermined due to a lack of flow and consistency. The best papers in economics are well thought out and planned, and if you are a naturally messy individual like myself, you will have to force yourself (and your study) to be 'neat'!

So, before you begin writing your dissertation, be sure to familiarize yourself with how an economics thesis should be structured. Generally, a typical economics paper is organized in the following way in consecutive order:

1. Cover Page
2. Abstract
3. Acknowledgments

   * *Points 1 to 3 are usually on 1 page (i.e. the same page)*

4. Contents Page
5. Introduction
6. Literature Review and Background Information

7. Data
8. Empirical Method
9. Results
10. Robustness Checks
11. Conclusion
12. Appendix A: Figures
13. Appendix B: Tables
14. References

I would recommend sticking to this format for the organization of your economics dissertation and include all sections listed above. This structure is standard and is used by many economics studies, so little could go wrong if you do the same.

Of course, feel free to add subheadings and subsections, wherever relevant for your study. In fact, you SHOULD add subsections as they help to break down your paper for the reader to follow easily. Remember that the organization of your study is just like the skeletal system. Without good support and structure, you cannot have a well-written and coherent economics dissertation.

CHAPTER 6

INTRODUCTION

The introduction of your economics dissertation is *one of the last sections that I advise students to write*. Of course, ultimately, in what order you want to write your thesis is entirely up to you. But, why do I suggest writing your introduction last (i.e. after completing all other sections)? Many students make the mistake of over-repeating content in the introduction and conclusion sections. It is important to know that while these sections have some overlap, they are not the same, and too much repeated content should therefore be avoided. In essence, the introduction should serve to *motivate* your topic by discussing how and why your research question is important for policy. On the other hand, the conclusion should *summarize* your main findings and briefly discuss policy implications.

One of the main reasons why I recommend that students leave the introduction to the last is so that the content they just wrote for the conclusion remains 'fresh' in their minds. This is good, because it should help to reduce repetitions in the introduction. In addition, because you will have a much better idea and overview of your whole study by the time you complete the denser parts like the data, methodology, and results sections, you will be better able to motivate your topic in the introduction.

Typically, the introduction of an economics research paper should cover the following:

A). Motivation for the topic of choice/research question. For instance, why should one examine the effectiveness of cash transfers on improving the nutrition of poor children? This is because nutrition is shown to be strongly correlated with future educational and labor market outcomes, which should subsequently alleviate poverty. And, so what? Well, alleviating poverty is one of the 2030 sustainable development goals (SDGs) as it leads to long-run economic development and increased well-being of individuals in poorer countries. In essence, *always ask yourself 'so what?'* to help you write the motivation for your paper.

B). Summary of the study's unique contribution to existing literature. *This should not be confused with the 'Literature Review' section*. Here, you should only write a few sentences about how your study differs from others and its key contributions. For example, did you use a novel dataset or empirical method? Is your study the first to examine this specific research question, or in a different context from other papers, or is your paper the first to establish causality? In general, think about how to differentiate your study from existing ones.

C). A brief discussion of the empirical method or theoretical model. Again, you only need to write about 1-2 sentences about the empirical method of choice, and/or briefly describe your theoretical model. You should only go into detail regarding your methodology or model in the later sections of your paper.

D). A brief overview of existing studies. By 'brief overview', I mean *a very mini literature review*. For instance, this could be done in tandem with explaining how your paper contributes to the existing literature by stating what other studies have already done and what you do differently. Be careful not to overlap too much with your 'Literature Review' section, which should be much more elaborate and detailed!

E). A brief discussion of your main results (optional). In general, it is fine to write a sentence or two about what your findings are. However, some examiners prefer that you leave this out in the introduction because you are not supposed to 'spoil too much of the surprise'. If you are unsure whether this is something you should include in the introduction, verify this with your professors or tutors.

CHAPTER 7

LITERATURE REVIEW

Gathering literature to cite for your study can be one of the more tedious tasks. *A common misconception that students have is that they must cite ALL studies related to the topic!* However, this is not true because it is more of a matter of quality over quantity. This means that you should select studies that have been published in A-listed journals, and/or have very convincing results, rather than referencing many papers that have either been published in 'bad' journals, have not been published yet, or do not have conceivable results.

In general, it is sufficient to cite about 18-20 studies in your dissertation. There is no rule-of-thumb number, though 18-20 is usually the benchmark. So, how do you select 'good quality' references for your research paper? To narrow down on your references, use the following pointers as a guide:

A). Type in the exact keywords of your topic rather than long sentences. For example, if you are searching for literature on cash transfer programs and children's nutritional status, you should type in something like 'cash transfer children nutrition' in your search engine or university library repository rather than 'the effect of cash transfer programs on children's health and nutrition'. If you are still unable to find studies that you are looking for, try keywords that are closely *related* to your research topic of choice. Using the same example as above this would equate to something like 'cash subsidies health children'.

B). Check the ratings of journals that studies are published in. You can do this by typing 'Journal Rankings for Economics' in your search engine to see how well the journal in which the paper you wish to cite is ranked. There is no particular journal rating cut off, but in general, try to cite articles in journals that are at least in the top 25% of journal rankings.

C). Organize studies according to the topic in different folders. This will come in very handy later on when you are writing your literature review. I recommend using *reference managers* like 'Mendeley' or something similar that helps you store your studies in a repository.

D). Check if the paper has been published or is still a 'working paper'. Working papers mean that the study has not yet been published in a peer-reviewed journal and that the authors are still, well as the name implies, working on the study. Generally, there is no rule against citing these studies IF you cannot find any papers on this topic, though it is important to state that it is a working paper.

E). Think about how convincing the results of that study you wish to cite are. For example, is there anything that threatens the causal interpretation of the results, and have the authors addressed this issue? Are there any other concerns you have with the credibility of the results? If so, you should either state them in your paper or not cite them at all.

Once you have selected the studies you want to cite in your economics dissertation, you can use websites like 'Google Scholar' or built-in citation programs like 'Mendeley' to construct your bibliography section. Both are great methods, though I prefer using

Google Scholar as it is very straightforward to use. Simply copy and paste the title of the study you want to cite in the search tab of Google Scholar, then click on the " sign. You should see a list of references in different formats (MLA/APA/Chicago etc.) that you can select from and copy into your bibliography section. Here's an example below:

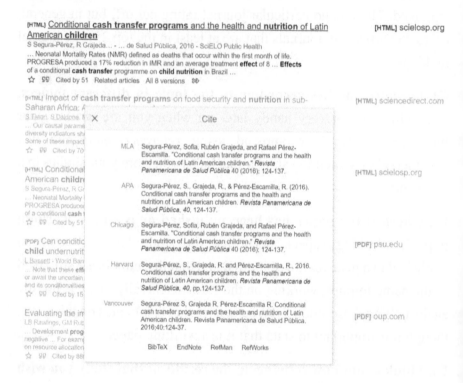

Be sure to check your copied and pasted references before submitting it though! Google Scholar can sometimes make mistakes with spacing, punctuations etc.

CHAPTER 8

DATA

O ne of the most crucial parts of an economics dissertation is the data used for the study. If you have decided to go with a theoretical paper, this section may seem of less importance to you. However, few theoretical papers nowadays omit the data component. Many high-quality economic theory studies often use real-world data to support their postulated theories and models. Therefore, *whether you have chosen to do a quantitative or theoretical paper, do not neglect this section*! After all, how do we know if an economic theory is true if it is not tested with real-world data?

A). Data availability. It is important to do your research about what data is available to answer your research question. Using previous examples, say, you want to examine the effectiveness of cash transfer programs on the nutritional status of poor children in Nigeria. In this case, you will need micro-level representative survey data on households in Nigeria that contains information about children's nutritional status AND whether households received the cash transfers. If only one of these data is available, your study is not feasible as both have to be present for a relationship to be examined. Another example is if you wanted to study the effect of immigration on house prices in the U.S. For this, you would need macro-level data on house prices in the region(s) you are interested in, and also information on the share of immigrants or the immigration rate in these regions. *Do not forget that any good thesis will also include control* *variables* that influence the outcome variable of interest, so remember to check if your dataset contains controls as well!

B). Strength of data. *Strength of data refers to the extent that your dataset can answer your research question well.* In this respect, say, for instance, data is available to answer your research question, but there are lots of missing data points or too few observations that received 'treatment'. Taking the same Nigeria cash transfer example as above, if there is information on whether households received the cash transfer and children's nutritional statuses, but only very few households received the cash transfer, and/or there are many missing data points for this particular question, then it may be difficult to elicit any results. This is due to low statistical power in that there are too few observations in the 'treated' group (households that received the cash transfer) for results to show (i.e. statistically insignificant), and thus this impedes proper inference. All in all, it's important to think about the feasibility and strength of your dataset for answering your research question. If data is weak, this will undermine the credibility of your empirical results and hence, your final dissertation grade.

C). Data cleaning. Once you have evaluated points A). and B). above, it is time to start your data cleaning process. Just like your literature review, this is probably one of the more 'tiring' parts of your economics dissertation. However, once you get past it, running the analyses and getting your results should be more or less a breeze. Some of you may not even have to clean your dataset because it may already have been done for you. But, this ultimately depends on your research question and the data source. *At this point, it is helpful to go back to your econometrics class notes on how to operate statistical packages like STATA, SPSS, R, Python, etc., to clean your dataset and utilize your data to answer your research question.* If you feel lost, and think you need some STATA help, for example, there are many online

STATA tutors and tutors for other programs that may be able to guide you through the data cleaning process and/or analysis. This is a website that I run that summarizes and reviews all available STATA tutors online. Otherwise, there are also many free videos about STATA and other statistical programs on YouTube that you can always use as a guide.

CHAPTER 9

METHODOLOGY

Your method of estimation or empirical model is the most important section of your economics dissertation. Why does it hold so much weight and significance in studies? This is because your estimation model will determine how your results are interpreted and to a large degree, how believable your study is. It is, therefore, crucial to spend some time thinking about what estimation method you will employ in your economics thesis.

While this may seem like a difficult task, choosing an empirical model is pretty straightforward. First, *think about what type of data you have.* Is it a cross-section, or panel? Second, *is your dependent (outcome) variable binary or continuous?* Third, *was there some sort of exogenous (random) event that took place (such as the 2008-2009 financial crisis, or a sudden policy change, for instance) that created variation in your explanatory variable ('X')?* These are some examples of guiding questions you can ask yourself to help you determine the most suitable empirical model for your paper, though this list is not exhaustive.

In this section, I am going to cover five common empirical methods at the undergraduate economics level: 1). Difference-in-differences/Fixed Effects, 2). OLS, 3). Pooled OLS, 4). Probit/Logit, and 5). Instrumental Variables. However, since this is not a book about econometric theory, I will not be going into detail about the technical aspects of these models but rather the practical uses of these methods in economics. If you have not covered any one of these models in your econometrics class, feel free to skip them. Depending on your university and curriculum, your professor may or may not have gone through some of these methods. In addition, some universities may have gone through other econometric methods not covered in this section, so be sure to consider them as well. Lastly, please *remember to write out your estimation equation early on at the beginning of your methodology section*!

1). Difference-in-Differences/Fixed Effects Model

Difference-in-differences (D-I-D) is often integrated with the Fixed Effects model and is one of the most popular econometric strategies employed in empirical papers, and for good reason. Depending on the data available, D-I-D estimation can give very clean empirical results. By 'clean', I mean results that can be causally interpreted. Essentially, D-I-D compares changes in mean outcomes over time between the treated and control groups. But how do you decide whether your data is suitable for a D-I-D analysis? Use the following questions to guide you.

A). Is there sufficient variation in your explanatory variable of interest ('X')? *Does your 'X' vary over time and/or across geographic regions?* For instance, you want to examine the effect of homicide rates on unemployment in Mexico. Do homicide rates differ across regions or states over time? If the answer is yes, then move on to part B).

B). Is there a clear temporal 'break' in the data? For example, *was there a sudden increase or decrease in your 'X' variable over time?* Say, for example, homicide rates in Mexico were relatively stable on average between 1990 and 2006, but suddenly increased from 2007 onwards due to war (see Figure A below).

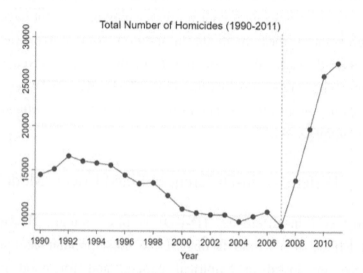

Figure A: *Graph of Mexico's homicide rates between 1990 - 2011, with the onset of war in 2007. Source: Author's own illustrations. Data on homicides is from the Mexican National Institute for Statistics and Geography (INEGI).*

If you do not see any sharp changes in your 'X' variable like in the diagram above, this does not mean you cannot continue with a D-I-D analysis. However, the data *should at least have some variation over time* rather than stay constant. Otherwise, a D-I-D and Fixed Effects model is not suitable.

C). Is there sufficient pre and post-data available for your 'Y' outcome variable? Using the same example above, is there sufficient available unemployment rate ('Y' variable) data before 2007, and after 2007? If you only have data for 1 year before 2007, and 5 or more years after 2007, you may want to be cautious. Why? Because having too few pre-treatment data points will make it difficult to test the assumptions of the model like parallel trends (see point below), which are in turn important for justifying the D-I-D model. However, it is not the end of the world if your answer to this question is 'no'. Very often, the availability of data is an obstacle for testing the parallel trend assumption of the D-I-D model. In this case, you should try to find other ways to justify the use of a D-I-D setup (i.e. draw from other similar studies, discuss the possibilities of the control and treatment group following similar trends before treatment, etc.).

D). Does the data satisfy the parallel or common trend assumption? As previously mentioned, this is a key assumption to the D-I-D setup, and showing that this assumption is satisfied is extremely important for the validity of a D-I-D estimation. *The parallel trend assumption essentially means that in the absence of treatment (say, for example, a war), the outcome variable ('Y') which is the unemployment rate, follows the same trend for both the treated and control group.* Here, the treated group would be those living in more violent regions with high homicide rates, and individuals living in relatively less violent regions with lower homicide rates would be the control group.

Figure B below illustrates the parallel trend assumption. You see that in the pre-violence period between 2005-2006, the unemployment rate for both treated and control groups followed similar trends ('parallel trends'). After the onset of the war in 2007 however, unemployment rates for both groups started to diverge in the post-war period between 2009-2011. The bottom line is that for the D-I-D model to be valid, you should be able to show that the explanatory variable of interest, in this case, the homicide rates, followed similar paths. Ultimately, going back to point C). above, if there is insufficient pre-treatment data, or if you are unable to show that this assumption holds, you must decide whether losing a few marks over this issue is something you are alright with.

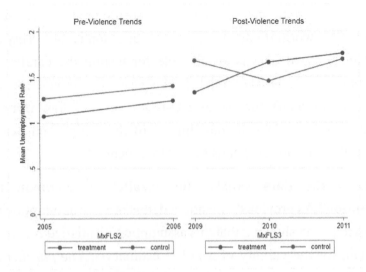

Figure B: *Trends in the unemployment rate in Mexico pre- and post-war. In the Pre-Violence Trends diagram, the top (bottom) line represents the control (treated) group. Source: Author's own illustrations. Data on unemployment rate is from the Mexican National Institute for Statistics and Geography (INEGI).*

E). Were there any other events/interventions that occurred that could also have impacted your outcome variable at the same time? Using the same example as above, imagine that a bad financial crisis took place concurrently with the war. Both would affect the unemployment rate, but since the goal of your study is to examine the effect of homicides on unemployment, how do you 'disentangle' the financial crisis from the war, which generated more homicides and hence unemployment? It is therefore important to do your research on whether there were any other factors or events that could have contributed to the sharp change in your outcome variable. If there are confounding events, remember to *control* for them in your baseline regressions! Otherwise, you should argue why these overlapping events are not likely to be a cause of concern for your outcome variable.

F). Do you have multiple cross-sectional data or panel data? D-I-D estimation can be used with both types of data, though it is most crucial to have temporality. This means that the D-I-D method hinges on temporal and, in some cases geographical variation to elicit effects. If your dataset only has one time period, a D-I-D estimation is not suitable for your study.

Note that I do not go through the random effects model here as it is less often used in practice because of its strong assumptions. However, for your economics dissertation, it is good practice to show results from both the fixed effects and random effects model as a comparison.

2. Ordinary Least Squares (OLS)

OLS estimation is one of the simplest econometric strategies to execute, though, in practice, fewer papers have adopted this empirical method over time due to its strong assumptions. This does not mean that OLS is a 'bad' strategy, it just depends on what kind of data is available for the study. *OLS is most commonly used in lab-in-the-field or experimental studies, with random treatment assignment and cross-sectional data (i.e. only one time period).* An example is if researchers want to examine the impact of cash transfers on the nutritional status of kids from poor households in Nigeria. To conduct this experiment, researchers randomly give out cash transfers to some poor households but not all. Therefore, whether a poor household receives a cash transfer is just like a lottery (i.e. random and not determined by any factor). The experiment is also conducted at one point in time (i.e. one time period). Under these settings, OLS estimation should produce unbiased results of the effect of cash transfers on the nutrition of poor children. This is done by eliciting the average differences in nutritional status of children from poor households that received the cash transfer, and poor households that did not receive the cash transfer. In summary, OLS estimation can be used when you have:

A). Cross-sectional data (i.e. one time period).

B). Gauss-Markov assumptions are satisfied (linearity; randomness; non-collinearity; exogeneity; homoscedasticity). This should have been covered in your econometrics class, so please refer to your class notes or online courses for revision.

C). Inclusion of fixed effects. Although cross-sectional data implies that there is no variation across time, the data might still have geographical variations. Using the same example as above, say that the experiment was conducted in different regions in Nigeria. In this case, you should consider adding geographic fixed effects (i.e. include dummies for each geographical region in your regressions) to control for any time-constant regional factors that impact your outcome 'Y' variable (children's nutritional status).

3. Pooled OLS

Do you have a *different* sample (i.e. the same individuals are not followed over time) of individuals/households/regions (or other units) for each year/month/period of your dataset? If your answer to this question is 'yes', then you should be using a pooled OLS estimation method. However, if the SAME units are observed across time periods, you should be using a Fixed Effects model as this is considered panel data. As panel data following the same units across time is typically more difficult to collect, very often, surveys contain different units across time rather than the same units. Popular examples include national household surveys collected by the government annually or biannually. Like OLS estimation, pooled OLS is relatively simple to execute. However, there are a few differences between the two methods:

A). Pooled OLS, by definition, requires *multiple* cross-sectional data. This is unlike OLS estimation, which requires only one cross-sectional data set. Pooled OLS essentially combines or 'pools' multiple cross-sectional data sets. For example, say you have three different household surveys for the years 2003, 2006, and 2011, pooled OLS estimation combines all three surveys into one single data set.

B). Inclusion of fixed effects. Since multiple cross-sectional datasets from different survey years are used to form one single data set, there is temporal variation. In this case, unlike OLS estimation, you should include time fixed effects. This could be in seconds/hours/days/months/years etc., or whatever time dimension your study follows. If the 'treatment' (e.g. the cash transfer experiment in Nigeria) was conducted across different geographic regions, do not forget to also include geographic fixed effects.

4. Probit/Logit Model

Another common method of estimation is the logit or probit model, which falls under the category of limited dependent variable models. In essence, these two models only differ in their functional form (please refer to your econometrics notes for in-depth theoretical explanations). *Otherwise, they pretty much can be used in the same situations, which is when your dependent outcome variable is a binary outcome* (i.e. takes on the value of either 1 or 0). For example, the dummy variable 'woman' is equal to one if the individual is a woman, and equal to zero if the individual is a man.

When presenting results from a probit or logit model, it is also useful to show results from an OLS estimation model, also known as a 'limited probability model' (LPM). An LPM is basically the same as running an OLS model, but with a binary outcome 'Y' variable. Again, I will not be going into the theoretical aspects of this explanation, but in practice, the probit/logit model and the limited probability model should produce similar results and inferences. Essentially, it is important to present findings from both models to support the credibility of your empirical results.

5. Instrumental Variables

The last method discussed in this section is the instrumental variables (IV) technique. To get straight to the point, in practice, *it is often very difficult to find a statistically 'sound' or 'good' instrumental variable.* Some studies have been successful, however, in justifying the use of an IV. Therefore, if you are thinking of using an IV estimation method for your economics dissertation, I would strongly recommend you refer to the IVs that similar studies have used. Of course, you are free to use your own IV if you are confident that you will be able to justify the use of it empirically. However, this is often a challenge, and using weak IVs could result in even more biased and inaccurate estimates. Therefore, if you must use an IV, try to use the same IV(s) as other papers to avoid more questions about internal validity.

Generally, for IV estimation, it is important to consider the following:

A). Is there reason to believe that there is measurement error in your 'X' explanatory variable? If so, how severe is this measurement error/endogeneity issue? For example, many papers use rainfall variation as an IV for economic growth in Sub-Saharan Africa. Because the aim is to examine the impact of economic conditions on civil war for example, and since economic variables during a civil war are typically subject to measurement issues, rainfall variation is used in place of economic growth for Sub-Saharan economies that rely heavily on agricultural production. In this context, as data on civil conflict is typically distorted, using an IV is appropriate. Overall, think about whether your 'X' variable suffers from severe endogeneity before using an IV.

B). Does the IV you intend to use satisfy the 'exclusion restriction' assumption? This means that your IV should ONLY affect your outcome 'Y' variable through your 'X' variable, which is the covariate being instrumented for. To elaborate further, this means that your IV should *not* have a direct impact on 'Y', and should *only* have a direct impact on 'X'. This step is often where IVs fail. Let's take the Mexican drug war as an example. Say that you want to use corn harvest as an IV for violence generated by the drug war in Mexico. You may be wondering, why corn harvest? To give some context, this is because corn is a common staple food in Mexico, and many cornfields were eradicated during the Mexican drug war to make way for the growing of poppy plants (which produce drugs like opium, heroin, morphine, etc.).

If the aim is to examine the impact of violence from the war on unemployment, then corn harvest is not a good IV as it does not satisfy the exclusion restriction assumption. Why is this so? While a decrease in corn harvest is an indication that more poppy plants were being grown during the drug war (i.e. increase in violence, the 'X' variable), it also directly impacted unemployment rates ('Y' variable) as many corn farmers lost their livelihoods. Therefore, corn harvest does not predict unemployment *solely* through violence, as it is a direct indicator of unemployment on its own. Ultimately, there is no formal test for the exclusion restriction assumption. Therefore, you must justify as much as you can using economic theory, why it is conceivable that the assumption is not violated.

CHAPTER 10

ANALYSIS AND RESULTS

O nce you are done with your data cleaning process, you're now ready to run regression analyses. Students often tell me that this step is *comparatively easier than data cleaning and management*. Well, this is more or less true. Because cleaning your dataset means that you would have familiarized yourself with using statistical packages like STATA for example, you will find it much easier to execute the empirical models required for your study. However, running your analyses is kind of like a trial and error process. Depending on the results you get, you may have to edit your empirical model, which can take some time. It is important to note that by 'edit' I do not mean fabricate or modify your dataset so that you get statistically significant results - this is considered cheating and is academic misconduct, so do not do this! Use the following pointers as a guideline for your regression analysis:

A). Present your results in 2-3 different columns. The first column should include no controls or any other additional covariates like fixed effects. The second column should include only baseline controls. By 'baseline', I mean only include control variables that exogenously impact your outcome 'Y' variable. If you are unsure, then add the control in your third column. The third column should include all controls, both exogenous and potentially endogenous variables. You can deviate from this structure, but ensure that there is a good reason for showing your results in different specifications.

B). Present summary statistics. This is pretty self-explanatory, but essentially it means that you should show tables with descriptive statistics of all variables used in the study. This can be done with the 'sum' command in STATA for instance, which will show statistics like the minimum and maximum values, the sample size (N), the mean and standard deviation for each variable. It is important to present these summary statistics in your paper to give your examiner a better idea and breakdown of the variables used in your dissertation.

C). When running regressions, add control variables one by one. Try not to add them all at once. Observe and see how your estimates change as you add each control variable one at a time. If your results change significantly when a particular control variable is added, stop and think about why this may be so, how this could affect your overall inference and whether this is a necessary covariate to include in your model. If this covariate is important to include, then make sure to state that your results change with the inclusion of this variable. If possible, try to give a reasonable explanation. If there is good theoretical reason to believe that the control variable is not necessary to include, you can consider leaving it out of your model.

D). Check that you are using the correct commands for your respective statistical package to run your empirical model. For example, if you use STATA, have you forgotten to add certain syntaxes like 'i.' for categorical or dummy variables, or used the correct command for a panel Fixed Effects model 'xtreg'? In general, before executing the commands, check to make sure that you did not miss anything out. If you are unsure, ask your classmates, professors, or tutors. Your findings can change drastically depending on the commands, and your results are not worth interpreting if you have doubts about whether you have done the analysis correctly.

E). Are your results statistically significant? If the answer is no, this is fine. Again, stop and think about why they may not be significant. Statistically insignificant results are not always bad. If your research question is to examine the relationship between cash transfers and poor children's nutritional status, statistically insignificant results mean that cash transfers are not an effective intervention in helping to alleviate malnutrition among poorer kids. This in turn implies that other methods should be used, or that cash transfers should be given in conjunction with other nutrition enhancing interventions. In essence, try to explain why your results are insignificant. This would be a lot more beneficial than going back many steps to change your entire research topic.

Another suggestion is to check your dataset again, see if the data cleaning was done correctly and if the commands were executed in the right manner. A way to examine your dataset would be to look at your summary statistics to see if any variable has odd values or too many missing values and work your way from there.

If you still struggle to explain statistically insignificant results, an additional option is to look for an alternative dataset to answer your research question. However, very often, data is not widely available, so this may not be a feasible option for most students, though it is still worth a try.

F). Clearly describe your results. Discuss the magnitude of the estimate (the value of the coefficient), the statistical significance (not significant, or significant at the 1%, 5%, 10% level), and the sign of the estimate (negative or positive). Provide explanations for your results, by thinking about the *mechanisms* or *channels* through which your 'X' affected your 'Y'. For example, why are cash transfers not effective in increasing poor children's nutrition? Is it because the cash transfers are not allocated to children's health, but rather to education?

Is it because parents use the cash transfer for other purposes? To answer these questions, try to look into your dataset to see if you can test if the cash transfer affected other goods such as household expenditures, or children's education expenses for instance. An attempt to uncover the relationship between your 'X' and 'Y' variable will add depth to your paper, and hence increase the value of your dissertation.

In summary, it is not possible to know what your results will be before cleaning the dataset, and therefore it's like a gamble. However, your findings are what they are (assuming you have cleaned your dataset properly and have correctly run the analysis). *If the results are not what you expected, do not panic!* Think about how to work with them by finding reasonable explanations. If you still struggle to explain your results, think about ways you can revise your research question or dataset to produce a sound research paper. Remember that the quality of your study is not always determined by statistically significant estimates, but rather how coherent your paper is in explaining the results.

CHAPTER 11

ROBUSTNESS CHECKS

At this point, you are almost done with your dissertation, but not quite yet! Every good economics thesis should have a section on robustness checks. Why so? Robustness tests provide your readers with some perspective on how reliable and sensitive the results from your analyses are. For instance, would your results still hold if you used a different data set or a different time period? It is not the end of the world if your results change, however, this would indicate that your results are *sensitive* to the modifications made. Generally, robust results should not change drastically when any changes are made. So, if your results change significantly during your robustness tests, be cautious about making *causal* claims! Think about how and whether changes in the findings due to these robustness checks affect the causal interpretation of your study. Below are some of the most common robustness tests:

A). Repeat your analysis with a different data set or another time frame. If your paper examines the effect of immigration on house prices in the U.S., you may want to omit the years 2008-2009 from your analyses due to the financial crisis, which could have driven your main results, for example.

B). Choose an alternative measure for your 'Y' dependent variable, or 'X' independent variable. Using the same example as above, are there alternative ways to measure immigration? Say that in your main estimation, you calculate the immigration rate per 100,000 inhabitants. However, as an alternative, you could also use the 'k-Nearest Neighborhood' method to calculate the share of immigrants in a specific radius/geographic area.

C). Run placebo tests. For example, say you want to examine the impact of a policy change (e.g. law that bans abortions) on fertility rates across U.S. states. This law was implemented across different states and across time. To conduct a placebo test, you could therefore simulate random or 'false' dates when this law was implemented across states. To support the causal interpretation of your results, this placebo test should show that the fake law implementation dates did *not affect* fertility rates.

D). Exclude certain groups of individuals, households, or geographic regions from the analyses. For instance, is there reason to believe that poorer individuals influenced the main results, or that certain municipalities or states are driving the findings? If so, you might want to omit these groups from your analysis as a check to see if your results will still hold *without* these groups. If your results are no longer valid, be sure to state that clearly in the dissertation and provide some discussion. Note that the list above is not exhaustive. The types of robustness checks that can be implemented vary from study to study, depending on the nature of the data and the topic of the paper. Ultimately, they serve to provide support for the credibility and strength of the main results.

CHAPTER 12

SUMMING IT UP!

Conclusions should *summarize* the main results and interpretations. They are not meant to be long, so avoid repeating the discussion of results in this section! The general rule-of-thumb for the length of conclusions is 1-2 pages. In this section, you should also:

A). Highlight the main findings of your study. There is no need to interpret coefficients here as it should have already been done in the 'results' section.

B). Briefly discuss what the findings imply, and provide some policy recommendations or suggestions based on your results. Using the cash transfer example from before, if cash transfers are found to be ineffective in improving the nutrition of poor children, what does this mean for policy? This suggests that other interventions aimed at improving the nutrition of poor children should be used together with cash transfers, or that cash transfers should not be used for this purpose altogether. Where possible, you should discuss as many *relevant* policy implications as you can.

C). Comment on the generalizability of your study. This is also known as 'external validity', which questions how much the results from your study are generalizable to other geographic regions or contexts. For example, are the results from your study on Latin

America relevant in the context of Sub-Saharan Africa? Why or why not?

D). Comment on the 'internal validity' of your study. This refers to the empirical method chosen, and how reliable it is in drawing out the main results from your analyses. No empirical strategy is perfect, so it is fine to discuss some (but be careful not to go overboard) limitations of the chosen empirical method.

E). Provide suggestions for future research. To do this, think about the limitations of your study. Is it the lack of a particular type of data? Was there another research question that was beyond the scope of this study that would have been interesting to examine? Drawing from these limitations or gaps in the study could help to provide suggestions for future research.

END

ABOUT THE AUTHOR

Edward Wellington is an Economics Research Fellow at the University of St. Gallen. Before that, he completed his Ph.D. in Economics at McGill University with a specialization in Development Economics and Labor Economics. Edward has also been a consultant to the United Nations (UNEP and UNRISD) on issues related to gender mainstreaming and biodiversity. In his free time, he runs a website that reviews online STATA tutors, after receiving feedback from students about the poor quality of private online tutors. Edward also enjoys converting his passion for Economics into artistic ventures and runs a pop-up online shop that sells Economics t-shirts and merchandise (http://econtshirts.redbubble.com/).